We Touched 1

A Book of Poems

Lee Alton Daniel

ISBN: 9798413018606

"Look where you're going,
and go where you look."

Clint Eastwood

Contents

Introduction

The sun, some 93 million miles from Earth, is actually a star and the only one in our solar system. The sun is hot, 18 million degrees, so I was surprised to learn that it had been touched. I read an article in April 2021 that stated that a U.S. space vehicle had touched the sun's surface. I thought, "we touched the sun" would be a great title for one of my future books. The sun gives Earth light, warmth, and the title of this volume of poetry. I sincerely hope you find a ray of sunny benefit from some of the poems in *We Touched the Sun*.

Tree

The tall tree with gnarly limbs,
stands starkly alone and bare.
The once lush green leaves and
generous shade are no longer there.
Fall came and harshly took away,
even the last withered brown leaf.
And leaves the sad silent tree,
to slumber through the winter's grief.
But springtime will return,
with warmth and copious rain.
And the leaves will flourish again,
bringing needed shade in summer's gain.
And with the oppressive afternoon heat,
when cicadas sing in the lull,
birds and human kind will find relief,
under lush shade, in summer's doldrum dull.

Disillusions

Youthful spirits are daring,
and their dreams are bold.
Chasing butterflies and
searching for the rainbow's gold.
But the butterfly flitters away,
and there is no pot of gold.
The fountain of youth is a myth,
and we all have to grow old.

Optimism

In the last days of the waning year,
before it saunters off into the past.
To be replaced by another year,
a new year, a happy new year,
hopefully, much better than the last.
But, there's still a couple of days,
and a few more hours as we wait,
to see if the new year brings better days.

The Family that Does

Christmas has come and gone,
it's all just memories now.
But what a Christmas it was,
and this story will tell you how.
It's about the Johnston family,
Mom and Dad and the two kids.
And how the family that didn't,
became the family that did.
Commercialized by big business,
Dad thinks Christmas is a scam.
Mom agrees and his sentiments shares.
And we know Santa is not coming to town.
For our family, Christmas is just another day,
until the moment we hear the doorbell ring.
It is Mrs. Jones, our next-door neighbor, saying
come over for a visit and don't bring a thing.
We hesitantly go over and find Christmas,
a tree, gifts piled high, and delicious food.
A happy and heart-felt Merry Christmas,
and everything feels so cheery and good.
Before the fireplace we sing Christmas carols,
and open gifts and have a great time.
And when we leave, Dad says to Mrs. Jones,
"Merry Christmas," come to our house next year.
And this is how a family that didn't,
now again, year after year, cheerily does.
All thanks to a wise ninety-year old,
who reminded my family that Christmas is love.

One Last Time

I got the news yesterday,
and I've come so many miles from afar.
To see you again one last time,
and to know how you are.
We had our sweet moments,
and we managed to touch the sun.
But your love burned out,
for I was not the one.
Today you're still single,
but tomorrow is your wedding day.
I just want to hold you one last time,
and then I'll be on my way.
I can see that you're happy,
and I wish you the best for all times.
But I know I'll love you forever,
and I wanted to hold you one last time.

Love Comes Gently

Under lush magnolia trees,
we stroll this pleasant night.
Along the river as we talk,
seeing across the water city lights.
Love comes gently on butterfly wings,
beneath the stars this moonlit night.
And words, like poetry, of a love song,
are flaming flowers our love to incite.
Reaching the second bridge we
cross back over to the city lights.
And now in the busy anonymity,
our love in memories must suffice.
With a kiss we part, 'till next weekend,
when again we stroll beneath lush trees,
with the scent of honeysuckle blooms,
and once more, love comes gently.

A Rare Blue Rose

Her seemingly eternal juvenescence
is fated, like a rare blue rose,
and all living beauty on this Earth,
to wither, die, and decompose.
But, by happy chance, we live in
temporal ignorance, thinking youth
eternal, and life forever, but no,
that flawed thinking has no truth.
But, no matter, it's a cycle,
constantly repeated in life's flow.
But know, we live until we die,
you and me and the rare blue rose.

Sunrise

In the early morning,
before the break of day.
To the east it's lightly pinkish,
while the rest is all grey.
Following a rainbow of colors
the bright sun bursts forth.
Lighting a fresh new day,
as birds fly silently to the north.

Mornings on the Beach

I love the early mornings,
as serenity lightly reigns.
Before the break of day,
and the sun's fiery flames.
While a few stars still twinkle,
and a light breeze from the ocean,
brings forth the smell of the sea,
and the waves rhythmic motion.
I watch black birds silently fly,
in search of unknown climes,
while I've found my place,
on a sandy beach at morning time.

Night Comes Softly

A warm evening silently comes,
falling like petals on soft velvet.
Lightly, comfortably, softly calling,
falling into dreamy starry night.
An evening of diamond-like stars,
twinkle and shine against black marble skies.
And as the night aroma hints of honeysuckle,
I watch, in reverence and awe, the moon rise.
Love comes softly on summer nights,
as a gentle breeze ruffles your soft brown hair.
The moon, the stars, your eyes shine brightly,
as your perfume sugars the nocturnal air.
And there, far beyond forever,
on this calm evening softly come,
I'll love you forever, as I do now,
as our two hearts, beat as one.

She Rises in the Morning

Through the open window softly steals,
morning air smelling of jasmine flowers.
And hearing from the windowsill a bird song,
after an early morning springtime shower,
she opens her brown eyes and stretches,
and rises from her soft bed of satin sheets.
Going to the open window, she views her garden,
of fountains and beautiful flowers lush and deep.
She takes a deep breath of clean fresh air and,
with deep appreciation, she happily sighs and,
bestowing a kiss upon her sleeping prince charming,
she goes for a morning stroll, in her earthly paradise.

She Walks in Yellow Dress

I met her there on the square,
of a small rural Texas Town.
Wearing a summer yellow dress,
that made me stop and turn around.
But much to my surprise,
she was nowhere to be seen.
I searched all the shops around the square,
until a kind old lady intervened.
Are you looking for a young woman?
who walks alone in yellow dress.
Yes, I reply, but, she disappeared.
Well, I'll tell you if you haven't guessed.
She's a ghost of our little town,
the woman that you saw here today.
She appears and walks in yellow dress,
and then quickly fades away.

Angels

She's an angel in disguise.
No mortal could be this sweet.
She's so pretty and intelligent,
the best woman I'd ever hope to meet.
We danced beneath the moonlight,
and talked until the new day.
I cooked the eggs and bacon,
she the biscuits and coffee, and by the way,
during breakfast she said with a smile,
listen and don't forget, angels do exist,
and you'll soon meet a mortal one.
To my surprise, before my eyes, she vanished.
And where she was seated, I found a note that
reads, I have a twin sister, just like me,
and I know you're her perfect match.
You passed my tests, now wait and see.
And sure enough, in two days time,
I meet my beautiful future wife.
who tells me she has a twin sister,
who tragically had lost her life,
and like I was told that morning,
and something that I will never forget,
angels are in Heaven and mortal ones exist.
Yes, mortal angels, like my wife, do exist.

Morning Colors

In the pre-dawn darkness,
the sky turns from black to grey.
And there to the east,
it's pinkish, before the break of day.
The sun suddenly appears, slowly
rising all golden, golden red.
The grey-black clouds softly turn
from pinkish to greyish black,
and then white, with the rising morning burn.
Slowly, but inexorably, the sky, like thru a prism,
changes from night black to morning grey,
and then blue, when the sun has risen.
This morning beauty many never see,
the pretty morning colors of the sky.
But it's well worth an early pre-dawn rise.
Try it one morning and you'll see why.

In Love Tonight

All the angels in Heaven,
must be smiling down tonight.
As we stroll along in love,
under God's bright starry night.
There are signs in the skies,
Heaven is smiling tonight.
Each star seems to celebrate,
finding love this star-filled night.
We two, so deeply in love,
this jasmine sweetened night,
and as each star shines,
we're happy in love tonight.
Each star shining so brightly,
like diamonds show heaven's delight.
and God in all his glory,
is happy we're in love tonight.

Evening Lilacs

Lilacs sweeten the evening air,
under a coal black marble sky,
lighted by diamond-like stars,
to count them, too many to try.
I choose just one, Venus perhaps,
and wonder if you see it too.
And if you miss me half as much,
as my aching heart misses you.
A new job took you to LA,
far from these clear big Texas skies,
and though we do communicate,
our texts just do not suffice.
Then, like a flash, it comes to me,
call and ask you to scan the sky,
and look at Venus while I do,
so we'll be bonded, you and I.
And all across the universe,
looking at the same twinkling star,
somehow, we'll feel close together,
despite being apart so far.
And the scent of lilacs tonight,
and as we talk the night away,
I find needed comfort knowing,
that you're just a quick glance away.

Quiet Mornings

Softly, in the early mornings,
when all is whisper quiet,
I stroll along the sandy beach,
while all the world seems right.
High in grey skies, birds silently fly,
as waves rush in and back over the strand,
before the dark in the east turns pink,
before the seagulls circle the sand.
Contemplative times to replenish the soul,
these quiet moments in lives of strife.
A restorative time to buoy us on,
in a world of more time than life.

From Dawn 'Till Dusk

We watch the sunrise,
with hopeful anticipation.
After a night of rest.
Then we live our day,
as the hours slip away.
What splendor, the sunset.
A quiet time of satisfaction,
knowing we did our best.
Morning suns burst forth brightly,
lighting and warming the world.
Giving us the chance to live or die,
in a brand-new life unfurled.
At day's close, the golden red sun
inexorably falls beyond the horizon,
leaving daily, a beautiful goodbye,
in the sky to the west, when day's done.
And we should be so fortunate,
to thusly end our final day,
leaving a beautiful ending,
as we slowly fade away.

Cold Windy Day

Today it's cold, bitter cold,
and light snow covers the ground,
and with a howling north wind,
the flurries come twirling down.
But, we're warm inside,
and watch through the window,
the windy, cold, and snowy outside,
as we drink our hot cocoa.

The Long and Short
of Getting Old

You know you're getting old
when your past is longer
than your future.
Looking back all you see
is past that goes on and on,
and distantly disappears
in the early misty unknown.
And there, looking ahead,
the future ends in a short time,
and from there on the great unknown.

Texas Wintertime

It's a quiet winter afternoon,
not a cloud in a bright blue sky,
while all across the north,
it's cold with snow and ice.
In Texas it can get cold,
for maybe, a day or two,
but, soon we're out doing,
the things we always do.
In shorts and sunglasses,
a tee, and sockless shoes.
We feel sorry for you guys,
struggling in winter as you do.
We touch the sun in summer,
and live in water and shade.
But the winter is sunny and mellow,
except for just a few random days.
Texas is a big friendly state,
and there's always room for you.
Just leave the winter there, and
come see why we love Texas as we do.

The Old Tree

The old tree in summer,
was full of life and full of leaves.
But, here in mid-winter,
it's sad and barren, with not one leaf.
The memory is still there,
and the promise is too.
That with sun and rain in spring,
there'll be new buds and leaves anew.

The Dormant Valley

There, the once verdant valley,
now seems to be sleeping,
resting the winter through,
'till the spring comes creeping,
in early trickles of water from the hills,
as winter snow melts in spring,
with the return of green grass and daffodils,
that springtime will bring.
The lazy brook will babble and flow,
as bees buzz from flower to flower,
and beavers, fish, and fowl,
will again have their summer hour.

From Sunrise to Sunset

Exuberant youth springs from the sunrise,
and from there to sunset, we cavort, struggle and die,
having lived and loved thru rain, cold and storms,
and doing so with smiles and tears, we wonder why.
We find that life is a long and narrow winding road,
that slowly and inexorably leads to the horizon there.
There's no turning back, and time does not stand still,
we're all the same at the end, paupers like millionaires.
When finally, we reach our destination,
and closer to the horizon we get,
we're old and grey and withered,
as we fade into the sunset.

Early Morning Rain

Behind me, to the east,
just before the break of day,
the sky is pinkish red.
Ahead, and on toward the west,
lies a large silver wolf moon,
that appears and disappears,
behind black and grey clouds,
gathering, to hide the morning sky.
A few drops of soft rain are sprinkled,
as a light west wind picks up,
bringing rain that falls in sheets,
as the sun comes up but never appears,
like the silver moon that's lost now,
in this early morning rain.

River of Dreams

A lazy slowly winding river,
flows through a beautiful wood.
Trees and green grass border the stream,
this river of dreams, where we've often stood.
It speaks to me of an ancient paradise,
a golden time, long before time.
When love and innocence was the norm,
and all was good, and all was kind.
Then her sweet voice asks me, Daddy,
why did they name this river dreams?
I reply, they were thinking of you sweetheart,
and all children who are pure like this stream.
She then smiles and says, I love this river.
And I smile and say, I do too, and just for you,
let's go get some chocolate ice cream,
to show you just how much I love you.

Wishing Fountain

Standing by an acclaimed fountain,
in a famous far away land, there in the water,
I see coins, like the one I hold in my hand,
from wishes made by people from many lands.
I wonder, were they wishes made for good,
and how many of them came true.
And which ones we're made for bad,
I'm sure there must have been a few.
As I drop my coin into the fountain,
I wish for fulfilment of all wishes,
in this baroque Fontana di Trevi,
that were made for good, my wish is.

The Old Man and His Dog

On a street heading west,
on toward the golden sunset,
from an elder care residence,
an old man, with hat pulled low, I met,
with a cane walking his faithful collie dog,
that seems as old as the old man.
A friendly "evening," and a smile,
the two continue on, dog and man,
toward the golden sunset, they walk.
How many more mornings and afternoons,
will these two old friends have to walk?
They go strolling twice daily,
once in the early day sunshine,
and then, an amble in the evening,
always together, they live their decline.
One, once a mischievous puppy,
the other, a bouncing baby boy.
Now, weak and decrepit, man and dog,
but still strong in love, friendship and joy,
the old man and his faithful dog.

Our Star

When I dream, I dream,
out under the stars.
And I wonder, wonder,
where you are.
Fate intervened,
and took you afar.
And when I dream,
I wonder where you are.
But one day I remembered,
a talk we had one time.
That if we ever were parted,
we'd know where to find,
one the other, under the stars,
and now I know, wherever we are,
we'll look up at a certain star.
And always know where we are.
Now, when we dream, our dream,
out under the stars,
we just look up at our star,
and we'll know where we are.
And if fate one day allows,
us to reunite from afar.
We'll smile, while holding hands,
and gratefully thank our star

A Dream of Paradise

I close my eyes and dream,
a dream of paradise.
And in this dream, I see
you, walking in the night.
Alone under magnolia trees,
long golden hair and blue eyes,
and I knew then I was strolling
in an earthly paradise.
You in a dress all satin white,
and I called out your name.
I said I'll always love you,
and I knew you felt the same.
I plucked a dewy red rose,
and placed it in your hand.
I said, this gift of love is for you,
'till tomorrow, from a distant land.
Somehow, I think this dream is real,
yet dreamed far away at a late hour.
I flew back home the next day,
and I saw her holding the flower,
saying I dreamed you gave me this,
and I awoke holding this flower.